MONSTERS
OF THE DEEP

JOHN PERRITANO

red rhino
b**OO**k s®
NONFICTION

Area 51

Cloning

Drones

Fault Lines

Great Spies of the World

Monsters of the Deep

Monsters on Land

Seven Wonders of the
   Ancient World

Virtual Reality

Witchcraft

Wormholes

SADDLEBACK
EDUCATIONAL PUBLISHING
www.sdlback.com

ISBN-13: 978-1-68021-028-6
ISBN-10: 1-68021-028-9
eBook: 978-1-63078-335-8

Printed in Singapore by Craft Print International Ltd
0000/CA00000000

19 18 17 16 15   1 2 3 4 5

TABLE OF CONTENTS

CATCH OF THE DAY

Chapter 1
SOMETHING FISHY

The sun was setting.

The sky was getting dark.

Two friends were out on Lake Champlain.

They were fishing.

They caught bass. They caught trout.

The day was over.

It was time to go home.

The men turned the boat east.

Waves hit its *hull*.

The men looked to the left.

They saw ripples in the water.

Then they saw something odd.

What was it?

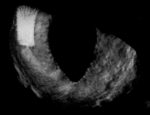

Was it a jumping fish?

No. A fish had not jumped.

Was it a log?

No. It had a long neck.

Was it a rock?

No. It had dark eyes.

Its body was green.

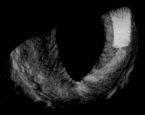

The men took a photo.
The creature dived.
The water splashed.
It was gone.
Was it the Lake Champlain monster?
Maybe.

Lake Champlain is big.
It's 125 miles long.
It's also deep.
One spot drops 300 feet.
It's a great place for a
monster to hide.

Many have seen the creature.

They call it "Champ."

Some have taken photos.

One shows an animal with a long neck.

If Champ is real, it's not alone.

"CHAMP"

Chapter 2
PLENTY OF MONSTERS

Sea and lake monsters are everywhere.

They have been around for years.

Some are *myths*.

Some are lies.

Others are mysteries.

They are waiting to be solved.

That's the job of special scientists.
They are called *cryptozoologists*.
Cryptids are *ancient* animals
that have yet to be found.
Some are thought to be *extinct*.
Some are strange *species*.

CRYPTIDS

A few play hide-and-seek.

They lurk in lakes.

The live deep under the sea.

A few hide in rivers.

Have you ever seen one?

Do you want to?

Chapter 3
OCEANS OF WONDER

The oceans are big.

They are deep.

We sail the oceans.

We fish the oceans.

We play there too.

OCEAN DROP

Do we know what lives in the ocean?
Not always.

Whales live there. We know that.
So do fish.
Creepy creatures live there too.
Are some monsters?
It depends whom you ask.
Sailors have seen them.
Priests have seen them too.

Early sailors were afraid of sea monsters.

They told stories about serpents and dragons.

Some stories may not be true.

Others might be.

You decide.

MONSTER MADNESS

There are sea serpents in the Bible.

Chapter 4
KRAKEN

A monster reaches from the sea.

It grabs a ship.

It squeezes. It crushes.

The ship sinks.

The sailors die.

The beast swims away.

Sailors told stories about
a monster like this.
They called it a kraken.
They feared this monster.
Was it real or a *hoax*?

The kraken was real.
It was a giant squid.

Giant squid live in the ocean.
Sometimes they surface.
They have a big head.
They have one big eye.
They have eight arms.
Giant squid look *fierce*.
They have two *tentacles*.

Giant squid have strong teeth and a beak.
Their jaws break food into tiny bites.
They hunt for fish. Not sailors.
They crush sharks. Not ships.

Giant squid are *mollusks*.
They don't have a *spine*.
They are rare.
Fishermen found one in 2007.
It was 992 pounds.

KRAKEN;
GIANT SQUID

Mystery, Myth, or Real: **Real**

Location: **Ocean**

Evidence:
Entire Body Found

19

Chapter 5
HYDRA

Ancient Greeks talked about a monster.

She was called Hydra.

But she was a tall tale. A *legend*. A myth.

Hydra had nine heads.

Cut one off, two grew in its place.

That is what the myth said.

Hydra was mean.

She was snarly.

The beast lived in a swamp.

She guarded a gate.

The gate led to the *underworld*.

No one could kill Hydra.

No one.

Except Hercules.

MONSTER MADNESS

Hydra's breath was deadly.

Hercules was the son of a god.

He was strong.

He was brave.

He feared nothing.

The monster spit fire.

Hercules did not care.

He sliced off three of her heads.

They grew back.

What was Hercules to do?

He cut off Hydra's heads again.

His nephew burned the bloody stumps.

The heads did not grow back.

Hydra died.

HYDRA

Mystery, Myth, or Real: **Myth**

Location: **Ancient Greece**

Gender: **Female**

23

Chapter 6
DEVIL WHALE

Sea monsters can be big.

Really big.

As big as an island.

Or so some say.

A group of *monks* found such a beast.

This was many years ago.

They were sailing on the Atlantic Ocean.

They saw a dark island.

The monks *docked* the ship.

There were no trees.

Or rocks.

Or grass on the island.

Its shore was not sandy.

The monks thought it strange.

But they were hungry and wanted to eat.

They made a fire.

A pot boiled.

Then the island moved.

It began to swim.

The monks were terrified.

They ran to their ship.

They sailed home.

DEVIL WHALE

Mystery, Myth, or Real:
Mystery

Location: **Atlantic Ocean**

Evidence:
Eyewitness Stories

Was the island a monster?
Was it a giant turtle?
Was it a whale?
The monks just shook their heads.
They called it the Devil whale.
No one saw it again.

Chapter 7
SEA SERPENT
OF GLOUCESTER

It was 1817 in Gloucester, Massachusetts.

A woman looked out on the harbor.

She saw a snake-like creature.

It was swimming yards away.

It was brown and 40 feet long.

A ship's captain saw it too.

It had a horn on its head.

The beast swam away.

It came back days later.

Word spread.

People ran to see it.

SEA SERPENT
OF GLOUCESTER

Mystery, Myth, or Real:
Mystery

Location: **Gloucester, MA**

Evidence:
Eyewitness Stories

They said it was a sea serpent.

A man shot at it from a boat.

He missed.

The monster went away.

It returned many times.

People swear they saw a serpent.

It has never been seen again.

Chapter 8
"NESSIE"

There is a lake in Scotland.
It's called Loch Ness.
It hides a secret.

Hundreds have seen a monster.
The Loch Ness monster.
They call it "Nessie."

Nessie has been around for a long time.
There are photos of a creature.
Many say it's Nessie.
It's hard to tell.
Most are blurry.
One was a fake.

LOCH NESS, SCOTLAND

No one has caught Nessie
or found its bones.
It might not be a monster at
all but an old *reptile*.
It has a long snout.
It has large fins.
It could be a lost dinosaur.

People look for Nessie all the time.
They use cameras.
They use *sonar*.
They try to record its sounds.
No one has heard Nessie.

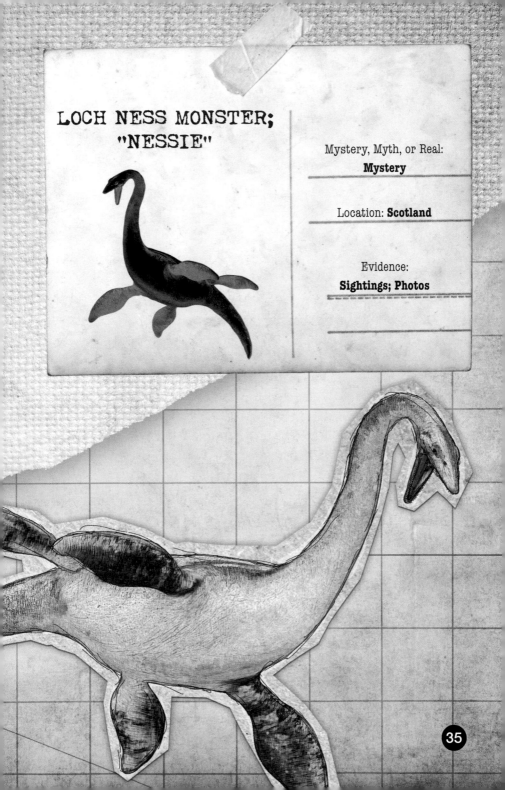

LOCH NESS MONSTER; "NESSIE"

Mystery, Myth, or Real:
Mystery

Location: **Scotland**

Evidence:
Sightings; Photos

Chapter 9
"CHESSIE"

Chesapeake Bay is famous for its crabs.

It's famous for its lobsters.

It is also famous for a serpent.

Its name is "Chessie."

MONSTER MADNESS

Most people see Chessie
between May and December.

A pilot once flew over the bay.
He saw the beast.
He didn't know what it was.
Many others have seen Chessie too.

CHESAPEAKE BAY

"CHESSIE"

Robert Frew saw Chessie.

It was in 1982.

His house was on the bay.

He turned his video camera on.

He filmed the creature swimming.

The monster was 40 feet long.
It looked like a snake.
It swam toward a group of people.
It dived under them.
It came up on the other side.

An *expert* looked at the video.

He did not know what it was.

Other experts also looked.

They said Chessie was real.

Was it a snake?

Was it a big *eel*?

Was it a monster?

People still search for Chessie.

They want to find it.

CHESAPEAKE BAY MONSTER; "CHESSIE"

Mystery, Myth, or Real:
Mystery

Location: **Chesapeake Bay**

Evidence:
Sightings; Video

Chapter 10
"BESSIE"

Lake Erie is a Great Lake.

It is home to trout.

It is also home to *walleye* and bass.

"Bessie" lives there too.

She's the Lake Erie monster.

Bessie was first seen in 1817.

It was dark and long.

Boaters still see Bessie.

It even attacked some swimmers.

It left bite marks on them.

LAKE ERIE TROUT

Once there was a reward for
Bessie's capture.
What is Bessie?
Some say it is a long fish.
Others say it is an eel.

LAKE ERIE MONSTER; "BESSIE"

Mystery, Myth, or Real: **Mystery**

Location: **Lake Erie**

Evidence: **Sightings**

Some monsters aren't monsters.
They're just animals.
One catfish is as big as a bear.
One jellyfish weighs 450 pounds.

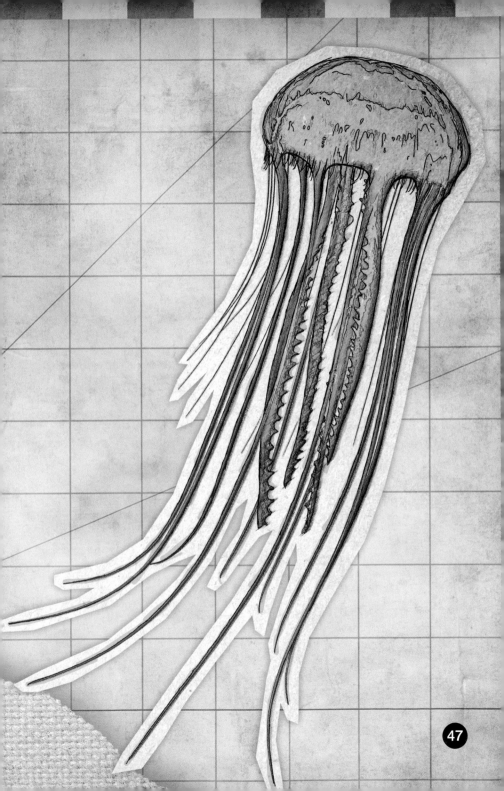

A few creatures could be monsters.
People have seen them.
They say they are real.

Champ

Kraken

Hydra

Devil Whale

Sea Serpent of Gloucester

Nessie

Chessie

Bessie

There are many stories.
Are they true?
What do you think?

GLOSSARY

ancient: very old

cryptozoologists: scientists who study animals that might not be real

docked: placed a boat safely next to land

eel: long, thin fish

expert: person who knows a lot about one subject

extinct: to have died out

fierce: very aggressive

hoax: a story that is a joke or trick

hull: outer part of a ship or boat

legend: famous story that may not be true

mollusks: animals that have a shell but no backbone

monks: men who live in a religious community

myths: stories told long ago to explain things about the world

reptile: cold-blooded animal

sonar: a machine that can find objects under the water by using sound waves

species: animals that are related to one another

spine: backbone

tentacles: long arm-like parts of a body that can grasp or feel things

underworld: Ancient Greek home of the dead

walleye: a freshwater fish with large eyes

MONSTERS on Land

AN EVIL BEAST

People say it's a *vampire*.
It drinks animals' blood.
It rips their skin.
It crushes their heads.

The woman is sure.
The beast killed those dogs.

Did it?
Is the Beast of Bladenboro real?
Maybe.
Maybe not.
You decide.

Everyone in Bladenboro,
North Carolina, knows better.
They all know about the monster.
They fear it.

Chapter 5
YETI

Nepal is in Asia.
People there tell stories of a creature.
They call it the Wild Man of the Snows.
You may know it as
the Abominable Snowman.
Most people call it the Yeti.

The Yeti looks like an ape.
It walks on two legs.
It has long, dark hair.
It leaves footprints in the snow.

MONSTER MADNESS

Alexander the Great heard stories of the Yeti 2,300 years ago.

CLOSE-UP

Why is it called a skunk ape?
It smells bad.
Like a skunk.
Like rotten eggs.
Scientists say the creature is not real.
They say it is a myth.
No one has ever found one.

But Dave believes.
He's seen the monster.
He wants to see it again.

FLORIDA SKUNK APE

Mystery, Myth, or Real:
Mystery or Myth

Location: **Florida**

Evidence:
Eyewitness Stories

MONSTER MADNESS

Some people think there is more than one skunk ape. Seven to nine might live in Florida's Everglades.

VIRTUAL REALITY
JOHN PERRITANO
9781680210361

CAROL PITZEN
Witchcraft
9781680210323

AREA 51
9781680210316

FAULT LINES
JOHN PERRITANO
9781680210538

CLONING
SUSAN HENNEBERG
9781680210347

SEVEN WONDERS of the ANCIENT WORLD
ARIANNE McHUGH
9781680210354